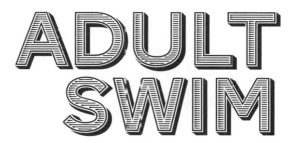

Also by Heather Hartley
Knock Knock

Heather
Hartley

Carnegie Mellon University Press
Pittsburgh 2016

Acknowledgments

The author and publisher would like to acknowledge, with gratitude, the following publications in which these poems first appeared:

The Chattahoochee Review, Congeries, Forward to Velma, The Greensboro Review, Her Royal Majesty, Hiram Poetry Review, The Literary Review, MEAD, The Magazine of Literature and Libations, One (More) Glass, Paris / Atlantic, Salamander Magazine, Tin House Open Bar Blog (in modified form), *Tygerburning Literary Journal, The White Review, Versal*

"Jules & moi" also appears in *12 Women: an anthology of poems*, Carnegie Mellon University Press, 2014.

The front and back covers are taken from plate 102 from the work of A. Ortelius, *Theatrum Orbis Terrarum*, 1591 (BNN, S.Q. LVI.G.37). Su concessione del Ministero dei Beni e delle Attività culturali e del Turismo– © Biblioteca Nazionale di Napoli. It is forbidden to reproduce this image in any way.

A warmest thank you to Dr. Maria Rascaglia, Dr. Marisa Spiniello, Dr. Vincenzo Boni and Dr. Maria Gabriella Manzi at the Biblioteca Nazionale "Vittorio Emanuele III" Napoli for their kind assistance.

Book design by Jackie Sipe

Library of Congress Control Number 2015945712
ISBN 978-0-88748-607-4

10 9 8 7 6 5 4 3 2 1

for Vincenzo

Contents

This fabulous shadow only the sea keeps.
—"At Melville's Tomb," Hart Crane

Sleepless Nights of Marine Life

At a party the other night
a lady told me about this
study she'd read that
sleeping pills cause early death, "Like
they lop off a couple years," she said &
I thought what about chemo or double-
crossing Hecate? That was near the
kitchen sink &
they were almost out of Champagne &
it was hard to get excited about the
sleeping pill study because she's the kind
of woman who would tell you that
sea monkeys are bad for you, for instance,
make bad pets, that tinkering with fate in a glass
bowl brings bad karma, "Like
you can't play god, you know," she'd say, &
go back to dissing sleeping
pills, leaning against the sink, metal bright
on her back, it was night & the moon
a mint under my tongue, later I'd like
to sleep, with my hair on my pillow &
in the morning rise with my hair not
on my pillow, but on my head &
I was trying to make the Champagne last
longer, & the doctors told me,
"Madame, rien ne vous est interdit," one by one &
when a doctor tells you Champagne is good for you, you
take them at their word because there are only
so many words you can take &
to the lady at the party I said "yes" a lot of times but
I didn't mean it because I like
sea monkeys & think they'd live fine
in a glass of Champagne, add brine &
algae, sea babies no bigger than a bubble & then—
I was so small.
Moon, I said, you blue
insomniac, move over,
make room for the rest of us.

I

When all your friends are sea urchins,

you don't have to worry about small talk:
nobody has a mouth.

When all your friends are sea urchins,
feeling "globular" or having a "spiny" moment is typical.

When all your friends are sea urchins,
wolf eels & trigger-
fish are not friends, but sea
biscuits rock your world.

When all your friends are sea urchins,
no one has a true brain & in the end,
that's okay.

When all your friends are sea urchins, the sea-
food is always fresh & no-
body asks if you've gained weight:
gravity is on your side.

When all your friends are sea urchins,
night never ends &
no one blames anyone for hitting rock bottom—
you're already there!

When all your friends are sea urchins &
when all these friends unfold like starfish,
because they are starfish, the invitation to
join them in the sea is no
more than a call for a huge house-
warming party.

Breakfast

—Utrecht, The Netherlands

Be sure to feed your love hard sweet cheese & toast and with black
coffee poured into round cups & maybe an egg, so oval in a home
of narrow steps, & be sure to spread the little diamond monster, the
butter, salted on your coarse brown bread, thickly. *It's okay to come
from nothing,* you see from the pond that isn't a pond outside the
window & those green steps leading up, with late winter on your
mind & olives in a little ceramic bowl in front of you & through
the front door come M— & S—, knitted scarves tangled in dark
hair, & laugh, then, lover, their laughter—*oh! you hummingbirds, you
firefly girls—*

"Everything tastes better with bacon,"

A friend wrote the other day, wondering when her butter withdrawal
would kick in & sorry for misspelling my name that once. It's OK, I
told her, some people call me Heater like they mean it some-
times. We're the same side of different coins, me &
this friend, & I told her there's a lot that does-
n't really matter, besides the butter addiction. You
should see it from here, she wrote back, from skies where
I am, broken with birds, some planes—
take this beauty, take it.

Some Benefits of Chewing

The other day someone said that chewing

gum is bad for your health, does

evil things to your stomach & a friend said, dying

probably does the same thing, & we agreed that some-

times what you want

to say is misplaced or outrageous or mispronounced &

people can get furious or confused or sad, write you up on

the bathroom wall or write you off into

the forked night, not that what some-

one else thinks is the center of your world or what-

ever, you've got your own opinions, may-

be you read Rousseau or Emerson in school, you're a think-

ing being, watched enough Monty Python to fill five full

weeks of time with the Ministry of Silly Walks skit at

the center of your apostolic

world & it's when John Cleese raises his leg & kicks

air, punching space blank with black-soled

feet, that you get it that

you got it wrong, your doggish slavery to what-

ever you're a slave too, even your potato chip obsession, or whatever makes a craving in you, makes a hole in the heart of your

dark night, like for chewing gum, Hang bad enzymes!, you

say, Give it up for Juicy Fruit, & you end

up having to admit that you need

people more or less & gum too, think

about it: you're at the end

of your rope & what do you

do, you call a friend or your mother & pull back a silver

wrapper & wait for relief, release, some kind of week-

end away from your own thoughts, & you remember

the gods, their breath, how they spat storms over seas,

were known to kidnap now & then, rape up

in a cloud, mess with hyacinths, slice off heads,

laugh thunder laughter, bring some human to their human

knees for doing some wrong to someone in the Pantheon &

if Boreas and Zephyrus had had gum, things would have been different,

wind sweeter, more pure & pine, less loathing in

the ancient floating world.

This other friend says, gum is totally plastic, & you are like chewing it,

but it's more than that, you want to say, a much richer

pageant, in this realm where frankincense melts on your tongue, some-

times we need to make up some

of our own history for god's sake, let sweet spruce soften in the pockets

of our cheeks, life can be

abrasive & you need

some sort of sweetener, it's that simple, you say to your nay-

saying friends, they just don't get

the benefits of chewing,

that coil in moistened places, get

a grip, they say to you, spit that out now & you think what Jerry

Springer said, "It's not the end of Western Civ-

ilization, it's chewing gum," & about this he was spot-

on, honeyed sap tucked in your mouth, spear-

mint that makes you ache, that you keep hidden in your breast

pocket & you tell your friends this is a piece

of cake, this crush in your mouth & you

confess more to your-

self than to the wind in whatever trees, that

some things are easy, open your lips,

place this sweet nugget on your tongue,

that some things are sometimes like gum—

when you believe.

Patrician Pleasures

"Pandora's Box" at 4:00 p.m.,
A nap in cashmere socks,
Posh, posh, posh.
Mantras and foie gras and Pinot Noir.
A red silk scarf.
A house in the south,
The exterminating angel.
Desiderata, palimpsest, incunabula.
Penny dreadful.
A gratuitous act.
No cash.
Farandole, tarantella, pavane.
"I Spy,"
eBay.
The first wife,
War and Peace,
The second.
A hoof stuffed in a slipper,
O my Machiavellian amour,
Patrician pleasures
Kill, my kill,
Kill my kill.

The Haberdashery of the Missing E

Tap dancing is fascinating to do with your husband or groom. Try
at midnight, in dark, on slick shiny floors. Try in a tailcoat and top
hat, you and your husband or groom. Waltz. It's dancing by moons.
It's X marks spots. Try tapping through nights. Tap
dancing, you know, stops insomnia and fights.

That baby with a top hat & cigar

must be stopped—
he's on the loose again and it's too soon to see his toothlessness,
that loon—he's gonna crawl away with another twelve months
in his chubbed out hands.

That baby with a top hat and cigar just keeps crawling back,
crawling back long after the millennium with its hypochondriacs and sooth-
sayers, speakeasies and Monopoly players,
crawling back through the groundhogs and grandees—
nothing keeps that baby down, sweet pea:
his dance card is filled.

And the book of hours goes by and the days too, goo bye, gogo googoo,
while we count out on our knuckles and thumbs 30, 29, 31—
hold onto your highball, he's here at our doorstep,
turn down the phonograph, he's teething on the welcome mat,
that baby with a top hat and cigar knocks at your door once
and does a little reverence—

Give a round of applause up to the gods
for the wings are full of confetti and young girls
and as the curtain comes down,
throw your hands up and curtsy or bow
kiss your beau encore encore
clap and then clap once more—
five, four, three, two, one—
happy new year.

Toward Some Leaning Near the Radio
& Those Waves

The birds are waiting, and the fish too, blinking under

the ocean, the sea, and that broken moon, no longer

cheese, that massive

hormonal cow hitched to it, just can't throw

her leg over anymore.

Singer?

Feed us—

To a Friend in a Strange City

Remember to drink liquids. To go to class. To say please and thank you as much as you possibly can. To find out the name of those delicious trees outside your window that scent the night with fruits and wings. Remember not to drink too much. To button your shirt. Remember to dot your i's—a portrait of the self on the head of a pin. Remember this, remember that. Remember that beyond the broken casing of your window in the empty square below is the bust of a hollow-eyed man, near night trees that speak to you. Answer back in clouds and stars.

If you can read this,

you're in range, the sign said,
and the guy standing near the sign, shirtless, in his front
yard, really meant it, and me and my Mom were in the car and we
were just coming back from the airport and it was sunny and we were in
range and she said, "Look at all that ivy, honey, it's almost covered that
house," but she didn't see the sign, she was looking at the teeming
ivy and a dog started to bark, his dog, the guy who put up
the sign, the one with two animal faces—his and his dog's—
get out, his dog eyes said to me, or maybe to us, but
my Mom was driving and it was sunny
out, and she was comparing his ivy to her own:
"It just takes over and you don't know what to do. You don't want
to cut it down, kill it. Don't want to do that. But how to tame
it?" She asked, maybe to me, to that guy, to his barking dog—get out
of here now, said the dog's face—maybe to me, to that guy, to my Mom
or to the grieving sky, luminous, out of range of any god.

II

Pool Rules

You could throw an amazing pool party—think of
your friends & acquaintances, invitations for
colleagues & comedians, visionaries & humanists & think
of your connections with the swashbucklers who
are always up for fun and often in need
of a new body of water, they could hook
you up to the wading pools of superstars,
you'd get invited to star parties and could
introduce VIPs to the swashbucklers, they'd prob-
ably love that, & sure you'd have to swab the deck & keep things
neat because walking the plank can be risky, not so
easy with a wooden leg (especially
if someone's been in the rum) &
by sundown they're all grilling & swapping
stories of Nereids, easy in their skins,
for a good time call 1-800-Ondine,
on the dance floor all your guests have hooks
for hands & it's hard to find a partner, some-
one ends up trashed on a lounge chair,
those Dark & Stormys do it every time. *Another*
round of ginger beer! The superstars might talk about Holly-
wood & the latest chatter about breakups, but really
they'd be more nervous about the friend of a friend of
a friend who crashes the party & that's okay,
they know you know the pool
rules & damages will be at a minimum if you stop
rum shots before midnight & no sword
fights or whatever poolside, for you are the prince
of this watery kingdom & with your arm you make an oar &
you row far, into the deep end, far
over your own head &
poolside you hear, *who invited the water nymphs?*
they're noisy & the last to leave,
look out, sentry,
adult swim brings out the thieves.

At the King's Party

January 6ᵗʰ, Epiphany, in front of a cake, France

In France, Epiphany is celebrated with a Twelfth Night cake, la galette des rois. Baked inside the cake is a lucky charm symbolizing fertility or good luck. Whoever finds the charm in their slice becomes the King or Queen and has to perform certain party duties.

With a tiny porcelain cow in her mouth, crouched under the table,
hamstring stinging, all udder and thimbleness:

Don't spit out the trinket, that heifer, they scold her from above,
until you choose your king!

They know how to throw one—a party I mean—
for this is the Fête of the Kings and this is the place

and this is who she is: *la benjamine*, the youngest one,
all giggles, diplomacy and sitcom stammering under the table—

we've caught her wearing a paper crown.

The French know how to party like this: name a few disasters
and revolutions, praise the high hair of Marie Antoinette,
supreme in a party dress, (sometimes) so easy to please.

the queen drinks the queen drinks the queen drinks

Choose your king!, they scream from above.

She never wanted to choose a king—
She's in love with a knave.

This Was Where It Was

You cld be the one I love,
when amorino, amoroso, shoes with people attached
pass, what do you say abt
walking together, it's okay
moustache moustache moustache
we can find a patch of shade
one, two, three, four, five, six, se-
ven, eight ways to say I do not love you
less, okay, then, it's hot outside &
that's okay too, water is good,
the sea, this is the same street where I find you
fr a picnic in the park w/ Nelly & Marie. When
you're ready, you're ready, he said, you
won't walk the same street twice &
then: Chronos takes big
steps, eats more then he shld—

On Several Desires & Entreaties At Once

If only the King weren't so freaked abt
being divine. It must be hard to be

sovereign in a hat like that, & some-
times, you think, & then think

again: god, it's madness, this desire, the realm—
his.

Rules sometimes are nuts & absolute
monarchy is overrated. You see all this walk-

ing down yr street & think:
I am the state, I am the state.

Gingiva

—Paris, France

Gingiva, she whispers and nods, in the know. *Gingiva*—
something between finger, jeering and java.

Here we are, Christine and me, at a little Sunday afternoon
party—a little too Sunday afternoon, at least for Christine, who
fills in crossword puzzles with her fingerprints. But her lipstick and
loafers are just so, as are, it seems, my gums.

I love your gums, she says to me, *they match your sweater.*

Yes, Madame, oui oui—they make an ensemble.

You can imagine the color of my gums: when someone says
I love your gums it's not because you've got the bubonic plague in
there, no way, it's just that *I've never seen that before*, she starts,
staring at my mouth—my mouth glued shut, for fear of exposing
those indecent, lovely, ungainly nubile gums.

She asks: *Could you open your mouth again? It's just incredible.*
She's used the polite form—the conditional—and frankly, so much
these days seems at best conditional, I open my mouth for her: *So
beautiful*, she says, *how do you do it?*

Colgate, Mom, god—

and you, Christine, belle of the ball, of my mouth, my maw,
spellbound by my gums, come closer, gingival dowager queen—slip
me your mandible secret.

Ode to My Right Tennis Shoe in Montparnasse

—Paris, France

O you, canvas one, where I make my home again and
again when summer comes—
dust, some rust and crumbs, I clean you
not, little one, but let you collect a whole city in your palmed
beauty. O shell, where my foot hides in heat, how
my love leaps to find you not
gone, not long, but right by my hand, dear
shoe, under my thumb.

Dear Vallejo,

—*Montparnasse Cemetery, Paris France*

Looking for you, under swarming clouds, magnificent, not
Jérôme Lindon mort le 9 avril 2001 not
Madame Pruneau in her stone-pigeon dress or
le Grand Officier de la Légion d'Honneur, or
the name of the man who broke up troops in Cremona

A friend stayed home, she wasn't feeling well, she didn't want to come out

Vallejo, you are somewhere among quills and umbrellas

A man in sunglasses passes by

Esther Lilian Abitbol née Gruez 1920 – 2001
Et elle c'est—
Vallejo, you are not
Monsieur Sunderland, not Blanche Saporta 1915 – 1998

I will die in Paris with a rainstorm
Paris, in a rainstorm, will die
Vallejo, you have worn your Thursdays out for years.

Mon petit poucet, my little Tom Thumb,
pursuant
Monsieur César Vallejo,
gone

Line 13 is from César Vallejo's poem "Black Stone on a White Stone," translated
by Rebecca Seiferle.

Jules & moi

"80% of success is showing up."
—Woody Allen

A morning of tiles, park benches & sun, green, un-
aggressive in midyear, with books & the runaway jury of girls
off to the Indian Ocean, Madagascar, to islands, Maurice, Reunion—
then the arabesques of black iron doors, 1 to 9 ABCD (you have to know), stun-
ning, this hour. That atelier is a red awning opening, *oh nothing*, beckon-
ing to an impasse where Jonathan, the ladybug, moves side-
ways toward Stanislas, just another name, proves
we are here, Our Lady of the Cars, the Fields—*Notre-Dame-des-Champs.*
To stone columns, where Madeleine meets magenta, (church not girl, not
my runaway jury of girls) as clouds part to Madura,
we move closer to the sky's crux
up & back to where we began, unfamiliar, le Cardinal—sun starts
slanting by tables. This just happened: dreadlocks, and who
is Gus anyway & why isn't he here with us—it's the last cut of the scissors.

Lifting Spoons

It's the kind of café that makes you want to steal spoons.

It's the nape of a Friday's neck, the first Friday of sun, of shedding, of everything.

It's a guy who explains what "rod" means in French.

It's about voice, that mystical, unteachable thing.

It's about beating your head in with a brick—

"Watch it," that guy said, "wild animals may come by."

III

I remember driftwood

—for Georges Perec & Joe Brainard

I remember making mud pies with friends behind our apartment
     when I was eight
I remember the crunch (very gritty) when we tasted them once

I remember one of the friends, maybe his name was Dan, & Dan

looking on, standing on the train tracks

I remember his high-waisted longish black shorts

I remember loving ceramics class in second or third grade

Loving it because the teacher was cute, Mister Smith

I remember how ceramics class smelled like baked beans cooking

I remember pouring hydrogen peroxide on the roots of my hair with

my friend at the beach, Nags Head, North Carolina 27959 USA

I remember running back from the beach to the hotel room after thirty

minutes to check & see if my hair was blond yet

I remember pouring more peroxide on because it needed to

be blond *that minute*

I remember *that minute* being divine

I remember driftwood

I remember our hotel & its smell of rattan & sand & rain

I remember seashells on shelves & mantels

& that big piece of driftwood in the darkened sitting room

No one ever sat in there

I remember American History Class in eighth or ninth grade

I remember the boy in front of me much better. (He sat near the front.)

I remember school Valentines & the Valentines boxes we made with a slit

on the top of the box for cards

My hand almost fit in there

I remember my fourth grade boyfriend: desk next to mine, to the left

I remember the Dorothy Hamill haircut

I remember loving the idea of her bowlish beautiful hair

I remember not loving the way it looked on my head

I remember the skating rink and, "All skate, everyone skate,"

I remember "shoot the duck" meant you crouched down and tucked one

leg under yourself with the other one out in front and you rolled

around in a circle in the rink

I remember being scared

I remember how good one boy was & how we all had a crush on him

I remember being tested for Gifted Class

I remember not testing high enough to get in

I remember they got to take Field Trips to Cultural Places &

Represent the School in Important National Things

I remember butane hair curlers

I remember the girl's bathroom at school & that particular smell of
    butane (strong)

I remember salt water taffy

that *that* was what summer was, because it was Nags Head

I remember dressing up in Old Western outfits for a funny

photo there with my friend. (We dressed up like saloon girls.)

I remember not really knowing what a saloon was & holding a toy rifle

The photo was going to be in sepia

I remember we giggled our heads off until the guy took the photo &

for that moment, our image carked down on our heads &

he swallowed us whole in his lens, camera obscura, down side up,

& I remember he

did it again & again, kept shooting &

we weren't dead &

we weren't afraid

What I liked best was the log flume &—

We're in for a ride—
it's the amusement park you were never expecting
sans s'amuser:
cancer.
Find your deepest sea legs,
now.

Fragments for a Surgeon

I

With your hands, one to the sun and one to the earth, we spin, and
the spinning moves and the moving waves and the waving beats
and the beating is the heart, the soft part that breams in the chest
beneath the black spike that must go, that burnt bark, charred and
ruined, that you must take back, that only you, dervish, can do.
Dance, dervish, be here with me. The bracelets on my wrist are
heavy.

II

(Because something always must go) and in this going is some
spring. Dervish, head inclined, (there is no stopping now) above
the spinning heart, you cut out bad parts with the scooped palms of
your hands.

III

There is the knife and there is the sickle moon. There is the closed
mouth and the stone open eyes, the yes, the constant ticking,
tambourines, daisies and the despised spike. The labyrinth of the
straight line to be cut, once.

IV

Let's drink together.

V

Your skirt flung to the sky, the night at your feet, turn, dervish, the
birthday of the day is now.

VI

On that day, our day, both in white, will be our wedding at the
spoken hour and you, kind sir, king moon, will take from me the
marred star inside my chest, take it from me from this day on, my
wedding day, dervish, and my family will dance, dance by the sea—

This Was Paris, France, and This Then Was Now

And then, they
saved my life—*saved*
my life.

Lutetia, Paris, Île-de-France,
city & island & bridge,
whatever name you want,
I'm yours.

Here, Even the Dogs Smoke

—Fegyvernek, Hungary

A bride floats by on a blue plastic chair, boiled chicken steams.
Waiters push past with carts of dumplings and drink. Midnight is
lost. In this light, the Hungarian flag looks Mexican. It's hot hot
hot.

Someone's pinched one of the groom's guests and insulted him. The
guest narrows his eyes. And he doesn't do a thing. *This is a wedding,*
he says and that was the mother of the bride, passing by in baby
blue, sheer joy and porcelain. *Otherwise,* he says, *I'd deck that dumbo.*

On the little back patio, a policeman stiff with drink laughs. When
he opens his mouth: swords. How we clap our hands. Here, in
Fegyvernek, near the Ukrainian border, even the dogs smoke. Don't
ask me to quit now.

Give Me Your Hand

Hungary was
broth and sweets and a feast at 1:00 a.m.,
lots of *nemnemnem igen igen*,
dancing, O.U. beautiful bride,
you whispering in the back of the yellow hushed church,
translating the priest, *You are entering a sanctimonious thing*,
sharing salami and breads in the car, picnic we'd never had,
driving across country to Fegyvernek heat late
at night, light from lamps along tables for
the bride, you & Laos
laughing, drinking clear drinks from thimble-sized glasses,
dancing & then—

In the Salon of Madame Miklós Radnóti

—Budapest, Hungary

"The road whinnies and rears up. The sky gallops.
You are permanent within me in this chaos."
—*"Postcard 1,"* Miklós Radnóti

She used to teach French, Russian, speaks about disappointment
in translation. There's a heat
wave outside, a communist
monument not far away. Dido, her long little dog sits
at her side. "Do you know
my Russian friends?" (She's talking about Paris and
the rue Cujas.) Her French is like yesterday.
I start to say, the poems of your husband . . . the war . . .
Have a biscuit, she says. Dido pulls her long lank
around the living room. Have a cigarette, she says.
We share one. The pleasure
to read is gone, she says, we will drink black coffee,
she says, I had long hair once, she says,
I'm a living tombstone. Madame, before
this part of the night is over, before I have
to go away from you and Dido and from the Danuba you
see from your rooms, before you open the door
and walk with me down the stairs, the doors kings never
touch, may I ask
we carry this between us—
the sky, coffee cups, chaos

* Epigraph of Miklós Radnóti's "Postcard 1" is from *Clouded Sky*,
translated by Steven Polgar, Stephen Berg and S.J. Marks.

"I was a girl in Hungary"

I was a girl in Hungary and lived on a flat plane. One night, fireworks went off and I lost my home. From the forest you could see flames and in between happy cracks in the colorblind night. A thousand firefighters could not stop it. I left with my name.

On a One-Way Street in Debrecen

—*Hungary*

In the car, we pass the *dinnye dinnye* and "the girls," he sighs. (Watermelon and girls, roadside.) It's August now. Every time it's August. In the car, it was so cold that I had to put on more clothes: his. Imagine Romania, the late 1960s, faces in fog. Fields at night. Girls expecting. The dogs. Dream your Transylvanian dreams. That time, my father lost his Swiss Army knife in the car. That time, I carried him through the gates of Budapest in my arms.

IV

You, unusual among fish, live in no aquaria

I

Sometimes people ask if I have children &
I say, "No, I have a houseplant," or "No.
I live with a Neapolitan," &
for most people that's good enough &
they laugh a little & then it's done because
it sounds funny to say that kind of thing to
that kind of question & only the part about
the houseplant is untrue &
you can fake that anyways but
it's harder when you said you could swim really well to
someone & you go to the pool together & you're
in the shallow end, you splash & hold onto the pink &
blue pool noodle toys because it's fun in the baby pool &
the thing is it's not exactly you're afraid of the deep
end where your fish-friend swims, because people
can drown in shallow places,
you turn around & they are dead, even with-
out the water that can happen & no noodle
in the world can save you.

II

Me & my boyfriend don't agree on everything but
some things we do, like for sea
horses we both think it's a good idea. We could live
in a Dixie cup with sea grass for a bed &
a little mangrove hut out back &
it would never rain because we live under-
water & eating cake would be hard but rent would be
cheap & the cup pretty weather-resistant & we would
find a way for our little family, because since we're here together
since that fountain where a dragon was dying in tagged up
stone, you've been around & it's not so
bad us not swimming together, & pretending
that we're not dead afraid of the sea, the haunt of waves if
one or the other can't touch the seafloor.

III

It's an innocent enough
question, babies. On the beach to-
day, playing catch, a little boy said to his
mother, "Pretend you don't
know me anymore."

Caffè Ristretto, with Amnesia

—Naples, Italy

Horns and shouts and mandolins. An under-thump of rap music and potholes. No street address—just sheets flying in the wind, white flags, drying under a ruthless sun. We're at Zio Toni's, *but that's not the name*, he says, *it's the Bar Esposito.* A scent of sulfur from up the street.

Our coffee is IT!, he puffs and orders two at the bar. I came from up the street with him, on the via of someone to get to this via of something else with its smell from the days of Pompeii.

This isn't really the Bar Esposito and the owner isn't a zio, an uncle, he says. *His name isn't Toni—it's Roberto.* Tiny cups of water in front of us, then two thimblefuls of black gems. It's that kind of amnesia on Sunday morning, somewhere between Napoli and Sicily.

He looks down into his cup. *Unoduetrequatrocinquesei!* Six seconds for sugar to sink. *Good*, he nods to Zio Toni who maybe isn't a zio but maybe Roberto or someone else. And he stirs.

And we drink. A sweet cake in two sips: small burning, then full dark bloom—

Every time you leave, the basil plant dies

like clockwork, I'd like to say, but nothing is like clock-

work—sprockets & digits & regular pay-

checks in the—how do you say dying stronger?— sun of early Nov-

ember when some drowsy gods crash the apartment. Today is

All Saints Day, that's what they call it here &

there, in your country. For us it's a farce the night before,

fun. Masks don't change the fact that the basil plant dies

every time you leave, or that after that time & the surgery it's some-

times hell and hard. What I want

to know is why all the saints don't come in & save

us, or at least the plant, or some apprentice

savior slip us an idea of how to pro-

ceed. I don't care what their martyrdom was—walleye or wooden leg or how

they hobble in plum-colored robes. Remember, I grew up

with Halloween. I like a fiend now & then.

A friend whispered last night, when we were supposed

to be listening to someone else, "This mess is about the New Year.

It's a heavy preparation." I take this to mean he'd been channeling

our basil plant, dimpling up in the fridge, where I cut some to try & save

it from the iron weather of Paris where it's 5 o'clock at 11 a.m. and no witching hour to look forward to, no

funny masks—it's all freaking day like this.

Even the candy corn is sad. Like clock-

work, you say nothing and I nod down & back

up, like one of those little wooden dipping birds, its beak slicing in-

to water back down & up—

Tip me over,

now.

Nine Lives in Ten or Eleven Lines

I'm flying down into my true love's arms from Frankfurt,
with fifty people on a two-hundred fifty passenger plane, night flight,
with three seats to myself, without having paid some bills yet—
that kind of grace and disgrace at the same time—
the way we live our lives.

When I want to say something devastating
it usually sounds like a perfume commercial:
mesmerized for five seconds then fade to black.

People accidentally die and give birth in the air.
And marriage? It could be accidental at 10,000 feet.

Night is a terrible city sometimes.

The Vesuvius, envious,

—*Naples, Italy*

One night, late, a wild dog barking in the courtyard, you wake up
and feel the volcano at your back in bed with you. Ashen damp heat
and all along the body, the cloy of sulfur—spiders and cinders.

It's a presence at the back of the neck, it's dangerous but you can't
help it. You don't really know the danger—the green below your feet,
the moist white heat. You've read about it and you've seen pictures,
maybe even in those figures at Pompeii.

You like to brag about it, the gritted taste in your mouth. It's danger
that makes you like this, that makes you big.

The Vesuvius, envious, that green bruise against you, is no dead god.

Chaos Is a Verb Here

—Naples, Italy

At the Porta Nolana, prostitutes lean into motorbikes, hunched over in late summer. Down the street, near their pimps, a man sells black lace fans with a Saint's face. You wave "no thanks" and continue— hands sticky and stuck with dust, dusty. You walk towards wolves on through Porta Nolana, its huge arch tagged in green letters. Yes, this is some kind of kingdom: you can rule here. A woman with pockmarked skin and spiked hair holds a baby in midair with one hand and laughs out loud to no one. "This is," you think you hear someone say, "a real bite of the boot." The sky blue of blue, stripped.

V

Who Will Provide Me With A Copious Fountain*

—Rome, Italy

Smell of paint and fried fish—oil and oil in an angled after-
noon, here's a fountain and there's another one, to-
night we'll eat granita—ice and crushed blueberries just start-
ing to turn, there'll be no moon tonight, a friend says, what do you ex-
pect? Now it's spring. You get what you get. Late night, back
at the apartment, a child is murmuring in the other
room. She has a unicorn, white with a pink plastic leash,
it's Sunday (still? again?), and the little girl says, "You see the Pope at
his window this morning? He said, *Benvenuti a tutti*, Welcome
everybody." That was not far from here, near fountains, this is
the water of Rome, take some, cup your hands and drink, drink
away, what you want, drink.

---

* Title is from Gaspara Stampa's sonnet # 136, translated by Mary Prentice Lillie,
Gaspara Stampa: Selected Poems, Laura Anna Stortoni, editor.

Toward That Sweet Nest Where I Remained, Though Parting*

— Rome, Italy

Yes, the saxophonist is playing ABBA under a tree, under sloping
sun in the garden of Villa Borghese, it's springtime, you see
this from the long benches and trees greened, this one has no
scent, when you want every-
thing to go away, he said, it goes
away, (he was talking to someone else), the train goes
the opposite way from where we are in the garden. The sound
of city birds first heard in Saint Petersburg over-
head. Then, there was time. In a supermarket, he sees possibility &
possibility tastes good. The young daughter of a friend understands
Roman dialect, Neapolitan too, but
still people don't make nice on trains. Under-
standing takes, the little girl said, time.

* Title is from Gaspara Stampa's sonnet # 161, translated by Mary Prentice
Lillie, *Gaspara Stampa: Selected Poems*, Laura Anna Stortoni, editor.

Ah, At Least Delay By An Hour Or Two Your Going Forth*

—Pittsburgh, Pennsylvania

On Semple St., a man in a bright orange cap stops, "That's it
for today," he says, this could be winter, breeze on streets,
sound of high heels NOW
HIRING, Pirates And Pens Available Here, We Have
Jerseys, Hats and Tees To Take You To The Ocean And Back.
Pass Atwood St., a block of sun, a woman in a rose pink skirt bill-
owing, a man sleeping, leaning against
VERACRUZ, FLOWERS, CHECK CASHING Love
Flowers! That was near Oakland, those flowers, across the street, there's
loose dirt, a huge flower bed, planting happening every-
where. Wanting yellow. Still on Sennott
St., keep walking. "Just the wind," a girl says, cross-
ing the street. "Yeah, they don't call it," a guy in a green wind
breaker said, "the motherland for nothing."

---

* Title is from Gaspara Stampa's sonnet # 59, translated by Jane Tylus, *Gaspara
Stampa, The Complete Poems, The 1554 Edition of the "Rime,"* Troy Tower, editor.

I Do Not Envy You, O Holy Angels*

—Pittsburgh, Pennsylvania

"How we gonna make it?" a woman says into her phone, under
the overpass, and, "Used to be
a lot easier than now," she says, and a guy going
the other way, smoking, says
into his phone, "Have to find
the biggest hardware store ever," tosses
his cigarette, and, "Miss her. I
really do." At Bigelow Blvd. and Schenley Dr., just
stop for a minute. The teahouse is open. "Pass
by that," and, "by there?" White, yellow crocuses
by a garbage can, you see: Happy Spring! It's tomor-
row, not today. This the exit?
It is. "We're building a play-
ground right here," the man said. "No kidding."
Coming late April. Such a noble heart.

* Title is from Gaspara Stampa's sonnet # 17 translated by Mary Prentice
Lillie, *Gaspara Stampa: Selected Poems*, Laura Anna Stortoni, editor.

Those Stars Whose Light Has Been So Impressed*

—Charleston, West Virginia

Greening in spring & some things are non-
stop, a woman walks right
in front of a man, (a way to make space), this is Capitol
St., a wide painting walks by with legs attached, gallery
going, from here to the shade & back, camp-
grounds close to forest close to down-
town, ivy stretches on walls, Dickinson St. not far, across brick
buildings, red taking sun in all hours, longer days longer, on
Washington St. E., a moving company
truck, *The Liberty To Move,* with stars on doors &
that light, hills behind & that world is the world is—
water way: the river close by, let's walk there.

* Title is from Gaspara Stampa's sonnet # 58, translated by Jane Tylus, *Gaspara Stampa, The Complete Poems, The 1554 Edition of the "Rime,"* Troy Tower, editor.

And Just As You Take Solace*

—Naples, Italy

Choose Yesmoke, world-famous Italian cigarette, re-
fresh yr idea of straw-
berries (or why not? calzone)—street food tastes like this. Make
a good price. Santa Chiara, we've come this
way before, plants with pointed stems, arrow
leaves up on the third floor, an inside court-
yard, casa mia, this is casa mia, and that's the Enchanted
Palace, you been there yet? It's a sure
value. On the street of
the spinsters, *Vicolo delle Zitelle*, a girl walks
by and her T-shirt, white and ironed, with cursive
pink letters, all curlicue, says—
un vrai bijou, a real gem.

* Title is from Gaspara Stampa's sonnet # 17, translated by Jane Tylus, *Gaspara Stampa, The Complete Poems, The 1554 Edition of the "Rime,"* Troy Tower, editor.

To Course Across More Kindly Waters Now*

—Naples, Italy

"Did this whole trip alone," she says at Napoli Centrale, train
station, TI AMO, Siamo at Piazza Cavour, Napoli under
            the rain & lilac trees, via
Costantinopoli, a massive sculpture of David in the cen-
ter of the stairway, high ceilings, "I suppose, *suppongo*," some-
one says, the sun comes out & the lady wears a coral neck-
lace threaded with a black cord & can give you directions, blue
sky now, pizza on the street (not just any pizza, *the* pizza),
Pompeii red arches & yellow, *rosa antica*, "this red is
famous," (old rose, yellow ocher), Galleria, grey &
white arches, a dog walks out into the street near the open-air
caffè bars, a woman with a long dark braid stares
as she passes by the bus station in front of the Piazza Dante,
and here is Dante, seven feet tall, arm extended over a wine bar, near
Greek ruins where Cavani, soccer player on a sticker,
            is a saint & then—
the history of art starts here:
in a stairwell with people smoking.

* Title is from the Canto 1 in *Purgatory* by Dante Alighieri translated by Allen
Mandelbaum, *Purgatorio*.

While In My Heart, I Feel The Sweetness Of It Yet*

—Naples, Italy

Near the open-air caffè in the Piazza Bellini, streets are slippery, red
Vespa with taped seat, laundry like white flags flying, starched,
a little place selling penne & mozzarella & fresh cuttlefish,
near the brick tower, there's a campanile, oldest of
the city, & a little dog in high top
tennis shoes near the Roman wall, & near-
by that a laundry line with blue plastic tarp & a fresco
half finished of the Madonna, in the San Giuseppe area
a woman carries a TV by out-
side tables, & underneath the tower with flowers on top,
a man sells cardboard boxes in Spaccanapoli. He
says, "O Decumanus! Our Greek streets!" And not
far away, you can eat al-
most sweet potato crocchè & calzone filled with ricotta, be-
cause you eat before you eat, & there goes
another bride, white before white.
Here, someone's always getting married—

* Title is from Canto 33 in *Paradise* by Dante Alighieri translated by John Ciardi,
The Paradiso.

Syrenka

I was at a job interview the other day &
they asked if I wasn't doing what I was doing what
I would like to do &
I told them be a mermaid &
they looked up at me like, what the—? &
whose stick is she trying to shake anyway
this is a job interview not
a joke &
that's when I said, Really, I'm not
kidding. It might not
show that I have experience with that
on my résumé, but some things don't
fit on the page. Huh, they laughed,
she says she wants to be
a sea cow, basically & drink
from shells. Like she knows what
she's saying.
I didn't think I'd get the job after this &
think I didn't want it to begin with but
you don't have to not listen
when someone tells you stuff, I mean they were the first
ones I told about this & it makes you think
maybe you think too much sometimes, &
that whatever skills it takes to be
a mermaid, I can learn them. You see,
I told them, I can swim & dive &
decide later about drowning the sailors,
sailors are useful & sometimes cute & not
every mermaid has to do that killer sea singing &
any luring I'd keep to myself. I applied for
your job because there's nothing tempting
about it & I'm good at hiding things. Well,
they said, we don't need someone who wants to not
be part of our team, we're about industry &
overtime, not sea cows. Don't call them sea cows,
I said, Call a name a name. I would not
tattoo *Lorelei rocks* on my arm for example, if I get this
job, I would promise to not
talk to the fish in the fish tank too much & not

wear revealing miniskirts, *oh, the fins.*
Lady, they said, we've got a lot of candidates to
choose from & we're just saying, no
discrimination in the workplace, but, sounds like you
would rather be a sea monster &
stuff & if you come here, we'd have to deal with complaints &
police reports, because, hiring an aquatic creature these days
can be tricky. It sounds like you're talking
about giving all this up, they said,
to be fusiform. It's not practical to not
have feet.
About some things they were right & for
sure I would spend time at work messaging pirate friends &
doing my own stuff, because some-
times in life you have to go in the direction you have to go
& sometimes that's straight to the sea—
your arms steering waves & onward, to estuaries
Syrenka, maid of the wave,
sun on your back,
this is immense, this is not somewhere else—
hey, I said,
look out the window & up, repeat
after me: rise, rise, rise.

Previous titles in the Carnegie Mellon Poetry Series

Venus Examines Her Breast, Maureen Seaton
Various Orbits, Thom Ward

2005
Things I Can't Tell You, Michael Dennis Browne
Bent to the Earth, Blas Manuel De Luna
Blindsight, Carol Hamilton
Fallen from a Chariot, Kevin Prufer
Needlegrass, Dennis Sampson
Laws of My Nature, Margot Schilpp
Sleeping Woman, Herbert Scott
Renovation, Jeffrey Thomson

2006
Burn the Field, Amy Beeder
The Sadness of Others, Hayan Charara
A Grammar to Waking, Nancy Eimers
Dog Star Delicatessen: New and Selected Poems 1979–2006,
    Mekeel McBride
Shinemaster, Michael McFee
Eastern Mountain Time, Joyce Peseroff
Dragging the Lake, Robert Thomas

2007
Trick Pear, Suzanne Cleary
So I Will Till the Ground, Gregory Djanikian
Black Threads, Jeff Friedman
Drift and Pulse, Kathleen Halme
The Playhouse Near Dark, Elizabeth Holmes
On the Vanishing of Large Creatures, Susan Hutton
One Season Behind, Sarah Rosenblatt
Indeed I Was Pleased with the World, Mary Ruefle
The Situation, John Skoyles

2008
The Grace of Necessity, Samuel Green
After West, James Harms
Anticipate the Coming Reservoir, John Hoppenthaler
Convertible Night, Flurry of Stones, Dzvinia Orlowsky

Parable Hunter, Ricardo Pau-Llosa
The Book of Sleep, Eleanor Stanford

2009
Divine Margins, Peter Cooley
Cultural Studies, Kevin A. González
Dear Apocalypse, K. A. Hays
Warhol-o-rama, Peter Oresick
Cave of the Yellow Volkswagen, Maureen Seaton
Group Portrait from Hell, David Schloss
Birdwatching in Wartime, Jeffrey Thomson

2010
The Diminishing House, Nicky Beer
A World Remembered, T. Alan Broughton
Say Sand, Daniel Coudriet
Knock Knock, Heather Hartley
In the Land We Imagined Ourselves, Jonathan Johnson
Selected Early Poems: 1958-1983, Greg Kuzma
The Other Life: Selected Poems, Herbert Scott
Admission, Jerry Williams

2011
Having a Little Talk with Capital P Poetry, Jim Daniels
Oz, Nancy Eimers
Working in Flour, Jeff Friedman
Scorpio Rising: Selected Poems, Richard Katrovas
The Politics, Benjamin Paloff
Copperhead, Rachel Richardson

2012
Now Make an Altar, Amy Beeder
Still Some Cake, James Cummins
Comet Scar, James Harms
Early Creatures, Native Gods, K. A. Hays
That Was Oasis, Michael McFee
Blue Rust, Joseph Millar
Spitshine, Anne Marie Rooney
Civil Twilight, Margot Schilpp

2013
Oregon, Henry Carlile
Selvage, Donna Johnson
At the Autopsy of Vaslav Nijinksy, Bridget Lowe
Silvertone, Dzvinia Orlowsky
Fibonacci Batman: New & Selected Poems (1991–2011),
    Maureen Seaton
When We Were Cherished, Eve Shelnutt
The Fortunate Era, Arthur Smith
Birds of the Air, David Yezzi

2014
Night Bus to the Afterlife, Peter Cooley
Alexandria, Jasmine Bailey
Dear Gravity, Gregory Djanikian
Pretenders, Jeff Friedman
How I Went Red, Maggie Glover
All That Might Be Done, Samuel Green
Man, Ricardo Pau-Llosa
The Wingless, Cecilia Llompart

2015
The Octopus Game, Nicky Beer
The Voices, Michael Dennis Browne
Domestic Garden, John Hoppenthaler
We Mammals in Hospitable Times, Jynne Dilling Martin
And His Orchestra, Benjamin Paloff
Know Thyself, Joyce Peseroff
cadabra, Dan Rosenberg
The Long Haul, Vern Rutsala
Bartram's Garden, Eleanor Stanford

2016
Something Sinister, Hayan Charara
The Spokes of Venus, Rebecca Morgan Frank
Adult Swim, Heather Hartley
Swastika into Lotus, Richard Katrovas
The Nomenclature of Small Things, Lynn Pedersen
Hundred-Year Wave, Rachel Richardson